TO ABANDON WIZARDRY

Matthew Caley's *To Abandon Wizardry* is his seventh full-length collection. His first, *Thirst* (Slow Dancer, 1999), was shortlisted for the Forward Prize for Best First Collection. He has published six more since, four with Bloodaxe, *Apparently* (2010), *Rake* (2016), *Trawlerman's Turquoise* (2019) and now, *To Abandon Wizardry* (2023). His work has featured in many anthologies, including *Identity Parade: New British and Irish Poetry* (Bloodaxe Books, 2010), *Poems of the Decade* (Forward Worldwide, 2011), *The Picador Book of Love Poems* (Picador, 2011), *Pestilence* (Lapwing, Belfast, 2020) and *Divining Dante* (Recent Work Press, 2021). *Prophecy Is Easy*, a pamphlet of very loose versions from French 20th-century poets, was published by Blueprint in 2021. He's read his work from StAnza in Fife – where he gave the StAnza Lecture 2020 – to the Globe Theatre, London; from Galway to the Czech Republic, to Novi Sad, Serbia. These days he is a tutor/mentor for the Poetry School and has also recently taught poetry at the University of St Andrews (twice), the University of Winchester and Royal Holloway University, London. He lives in London with the Czech-born artist Pavla Alchin. They have two daughters, Iris and Mina.

MATTHEW CALEY

To Abandon Wizardry

BLOODAXE BOOKS

ISBN: 978 1 78037 675 2

First published 2023 by
Bloodaxe Books Ltd
Eastburn
South Park
Hexham
Northumberland NE46 1BS

www.bloodaxebooks.com
For further information about Bloodaxe titles
please visit our website and join our mailing list
or write to the above address for a catalogue.

Supported using public funding by
ARTS COUNCIL
ENGLAND

Cover design by Neil Astley, Pamela Robertson-Pearce,
Pavla Alchin & Matthew Caley.

Printed in Great Britain by Bell & Bain Limited, Glasgow, Scotland, on
acid-free paper sourced from mills with FSC chain of custody certification.

for Pavla, Iris and Mina – perpetually;
for Jeremy and Inger, Evripides and Aspasia, and Petra and Honsa;
for Mhairi, in much appreciation and –
in memory of Bill Brown

ACKNOWLEDGEMENTS

Acknowledgements are due to the editors of the following journals, publications and websites where these poems, or versions of them, first appeared: *Bad Lilies, Modern Poetry in Translation, The Poetry Review, Poetry Wales, Raceme, The Rialto*, spontaneouspoetics.co.uk, www.thesundaytribune.com, newbootsandpantisocracies.wordpress.com

'The Vulnerable' was first published in *Pestilence*, a collection of poems and illustrations edited by Peter Pegnall and Gérard Noyau, published by Lapwing, Belfast, 2020. 'The Archipelagos', 'Depot of the Aero-houses' and 'Bollo's Brook' were commissioned for the *Divining Dante* anthology (Recent Work Press, 2021) and can also be found on the website https://recentworkpress.com/product/divining-dante/

'I Conjured up a Horse', a version from Jules Supervielle, was included in *Prophecy is Easy* – fifteen very loose versions from mainly 20th-century French poets, published by Blueprint, 2021.

Many of the versions from French poets owe a debt to the *Dover Book of Modern French Poets* edited by Wallace Fowlie originally published in 1955. And to Václav Z.J. Pinkava's website for the Czech version from Karel Toman http://www.vzjp.cz/basne.htm

Thank you to the Royal Literary Fund and the Society of Authors for significant help during the writing of this book. To Mr Andy Ching for friendship, scanning eye and precise scalpel, many thanks as always. To Pavla Alchin for the cover photograph and much else besides.

CONTENTS

every concrete object has abstract value, is timeless in the dream parallel

HILDA DOOLITTLE, *Collected Poems 1912-1944*, ed. Louis L. Martz (1986)

for in the book there is no question that Oz is real, that it is a place of the same order, though not of the same type, as Kansas. The film, like the TV soap opera *Dallas*, introduces an element of bad faith when it permits the possibility that everything is a dream.

JUSTIN REMES, *Film-Philosophy* (2013), '"That Man Behind the Curtain": Atheism and Belief in *The Wizard of Oz*'

Some say that knowledge is ho-ho-ho
Some say that knowledge is ho-ho-ho

KATE BUSH, 'Sat in Your Lap'

...under our northern latitudes, the gap between the duration of dominant, increasing day and the dominated, decreasing night is maximal until the sun arrives corresponding to 0°

FRANÇOISE HARDY, Clash Music Features (2018)

It is not for us to greet each other or bid farewell we live on archipelagos

ZBIGNIEW HERBERT, 'Elegy of Fortinbras', tr. Czesław Miłosz

always this worry
that manipulating stars
leads to error   that
to abandon wizardry
  might leave a husk   merely

  a human   just a world   which
cannot suffice   start a new
one out of a flimsy whorl
star-husks forming slurry   get
  a clipboard and a mallet

  see it as a prompt   a task

The Vulnerable

    everything forewarns
of this lynx under
scattered stars   its ears
like 'X's vibrating the
    Nerium oleanders

lint-snags of lightning

    fire   inside its soft breathing
in sleep downing a gazelle   with a nuzzle   all
    things being equal

The Archipelagos

   say that somehow you once walked
on the Archipelagos
each one like a half-submerged
turtle in emerald ooze
that each stride   from one
to the other
pressed each taciturn turtle
down a little – all
turtles being taciturn –
and once your step had passed on
how they bobbed back up
depressed lightly   un-depressed
with the same taciturn half smile
really not a smile at all
but a rictus   your forty-
league boots would flatten dock leaf
willowherb   belladonna   bergamot   brit
and unperceivably the
Archipelagos
themselves   with blissful
unconcern   no tectonic
plate inviolate   no crease
temporary crease in the
ocean   not straightened out
these are the Straits of Logic
the Straits of Increase   the Straits
of Sorrow   the Strait of Straights –
they are yours and you fold them
neatly into a known map
   and then roll it up

   and so   to the dog house: once sent here
hang and wait for a hint of
marsupial or straw
interchangeable as they are
by the spider house

loiter with the Latin tags
and fully fused animal smell
   impregnating the air   stay there

   the convener of
the Unconscious Bias Seminar
was biased towards us
   because we were unconscious

   everything else is whoops and strained calls
echoic against cool tiles
   and always for the mother   the mother

   say that you once walked
on the Archipelagos
and that everything furred
or shelled or feathered
   first blinked   then shuddered

Bagatelle

please   ignore these old men in black and white   stooping to
boules
    under dusty trees
the soaking foliage   the pollen count heavy
   as you affect to walk the points of a Great City
feeling as weary as *une belle actrice*
playing *bagatelle* with Françoise Hardy
   in your head   these old men   in black and white   stooping to
boules
    under dusty trees
   your heart arhythmic   so full of tachycardia
the defibrillating pace   of fifteen coffees
   shakes that slick   golden bell of hair   the severe slant of the
cardy
   as you affect to walk the points of a Great City
looking for anything that might spare you
   old men under dusty trees
the pollen count heavy   or playing *bagatelle* with Françoise Hardy
you will weep for the *noblesse*   the *noblesse oblige*
   of a vanished epoch or age

   as if setting siege to the turrets of a Great City
with the sparks off a worn boot heel   *sui generis*
– for the melancholic and the mardy –

   ignore these old men in black and white   stooping to *boules*
under dusty trees
   the foliage soaking   you playing bagatelle
    with Françoise Hardy   *please*

The Nit Pickers

(after Arthur Rimbaud)

    firstly   if any angelic brat's forehead
is red-pitted   red-dotted
with pain points
it will be this forehead that thinks
two sisters
all firm fingers and fly girl nails
who lead him to the sill
of the ginormous bay window
above a terrace choked with cornflowers
so blue they dye the air
blue   their tangle matching exactly the tangle of his hair
through which giggling fingers
      force and find and
as they do   he sees their breathing
   goes deeper into that breath   the garden exhaling
rose spores
and honey pollen   [the cause
of the reddening?]   low whispers
from lips as if offering
and withdrawing
a kiss simultaneously   feels the beat
of eyelashes on his neck – a hummingbird out-
      side an iris staying stalled mid-air opposite –
hears fingers which never tire or still
the thread of the nit comb
the fingers at the nits
the slim fingers dotted
with infinite little crushes
so this brat   as if high on the blush
of wine   seething with antihistamine
sighs in *Auto-Tune*
at their caresses
and under this tender head massage
   sheds his first tears of rage

Lynx Litter

    as I lay under
the Nerium oleanders   my hat at full tilt
too fazed to pull down the sky's
ice-blue canopy   or brood upon your letter
    – the one about your lynx litter screensaver – all
your emails accrued
    unread behind my *Normcore* grey screensaver
      as silverfish into silt

    whilst probably for aeons the demi-monde were
perineum-fanning on
    cobalt recliners

    in Luxor or wherever   O my days my days
        one day I swear I will lay
out under the Nerium oleanders   pull
    down the sky's blue canopy and   open your letter

Luxor

I

to see luxury
as a brittle   dry-boned leaf
floating cool   formal gardens
is to exercise
a modicum of restraint
    over a wild wayward life

Uxor   uxorious:
an excessive love of home
    and of one's wife   without stint

II

if this pain in the thorax
is predetermination
our days of orgy over
I will fold my ex-
odalisques in wreathes of *kif*
    keep them 'neath the sofa where

the heteronormative
is a cool formal garden
    to be left unattended

III

Luxor: where a long-haired mule
chews fronds of filter-palm and
so secretes a fauve-esque foam
we recommend exercise
to lie on   this palliasse
    an Ottoman seductress

watch your long left leg
overextend its shadow
   as if observed by Peloton   inexorable

IV

   then insert sweetmeats
between the fourth and fifth rib
feel postcolonial   say
'*O feint friends   goodbye*
I relinquish my role as
   a convulsive fumarole

   O goodbye my sweet long–haired
mule   I have already hired
   that roof terrace in Luxor'

The Blunderbuss

I

    if these chaffinches
do not soon alight and peck
the string of suet balls in the little mesh thurible
set up in our berry tree
I will break their beaks
the ungrateful trolls
or take a 410 full of
    Bitcoin and ball bearing

    and make them into
little chaffinch colanders
    the air will fall through

    and add again to air   here
with the feeder strung up up high   high and wind-swinging
I sit at the sill
    aim and never err

II

    the wind it is no clairvoyance to anticipate
                    in tugged gusts
has got inside our berry tree
is swinging the thurible
of the bird feeder
this way and then that
a terrible nest of noise
everything at an angle
    in a byte of pain

    maybe as much as you two
back and forth   an incipient typhoon
    wild thornbush and clematis   in a tangle
                    taking secateurs to blue

    to a heart shot through
by ball bearing   tin can and   possibly Bitcoin   out
    of the inevitable
                blunderbuss

The Leaf

I

you say 'there's a leaf
in your hair'   softly
as a tower block burns down
and mastiffs bite their muzzles
– put that in a villanelle –
The Ombudsmen are passive
as if treading on a cloud
The Ombudsmen are passive-
aggressive   or vice-versa   the crowds
   from up here look like stucco

and stucco acts as
the inner city's blossom
– put that in a villanelle –
some seasonal theme
   I am treading on a cloud

II

time is speeding up
we're gone   then return   up there
above filter-elms with their
aerial view of Shadwell
its tangled wires all live
you say 'there's a leaf
in your hair'   softly
as a tower burns [is this one Troy or
                Lower Manhattan?]
twist of security tape
   – put that in a villanelle –

a whole city is rewilded
in a nanosecond
as pollution lifts   no vapes
passive-aggressive quiet
   that leaf falls   [is remaindered

III

   not saved]   again 'there's a leaf
in your hair'   a tower
burns on in repeat
we are stepping out on clouds
like inner city blossom
one blink blots a life
the minute trumps the massive
some litter   a life   they say:
we hold a skeleton key
   to a lock filled with drizzle

   outside: muezzin-call and
siren–call meet mid-air   then mesh   as outside
a nearby shopping mall
some straining mastiff
   brings down a looter

   you say 'there's a leaf
in your hair'…

Approaches to a Door

(after Francis Ponge)

    secondly
there are
many approaches to a door
but first the structural one: before a door
there must exist a wall   then in the wall there
must exist an aperture   without an aperture
there would be no door
the former
a precondition of the latter
ergo – it is a hole in solid matter
that is blocked but not finitely   remember
the words 'imperceptibly ajar'?
if we concur
that no solid wall is there
for infinity or more
and find the line that is not a line of course but an
infinitesimal gap between frame and possible door
there   eyes slanting at an angle to where
on a traditional door   there
exists a handle slightly the worse for wear
this one   possibly broken by a passing vandal
    supposedly this being a somewhat 'insalubrious area'
somewhere to the left of Penge where
nothing survives for more than an hour
where
the kiosk's panes are
all lit up with asterisks   but where was I? where?
O yes   the door
[*princes do not touch doors*, remember?]
on seeing the handle apply downward pressure
pull backward then if everything is fair
this thing we designate a door
[no time for a brief rereading of Saussure]
will swing back out towards us   only there
and then will the light of an idea

fall across us   an 'L' of light fall on your floor
that you step into or rather
onto through or across   the air
outside being almost supernaturally clear
the fresh shock of a thaw
or the first kiss in eons from an estranged lover
spills sunlight on melt-water
as you walk through the door
    thirdly –

The Strop

I

suddenly to catch
Comtesse Dolingen of Gratz   near the Alexanderplatz
standing in a doorway
   her lips around an
infinity cigarette
its smoke in the filter-elms
down-projecting leaf stipple – projectionist the moon –
   onto those kerb sides   two stone bollards   to co-create the illusion of

   Comtesse Dolingen of Gratz
standing in a doorway
her lips around an

   infinity cigarette   blown smoke in the filter-elms
                smoke wreathing inside the crown of a filter-elm
by the Alexanderplatz   we watch it sway and
   wait for the overdue sun

II

suddenly then the strop razor
against my testicles and
grazing my perineum
as would make any initiate draw
in their very breath but
I see Comtesse Dolingen of Gratz
pining over a corpse in
   the Schlosspark Mausoleum

   as the Id pines for pleasure
and while this razor is blunt
   my mind is sharp with thoughts of Comtesse Dolingen of Gratz

as the filter-elms turn green
the people dappled green on the Alexanderplatz
    almost on the verge of love   there is no such word as 'can't'

III

    suddenly enters the antechamber
then   announced by a door hinge
wearing a shift so sheer
it leaves nothing to the imagination
yet through it we see a quincunx of orange trees where
Comtesse Dolingen of Gratz
on a bier   is force fed the juice of blood orange
                        after blood orange
    to keep her complexion '*faire*'

    two doctors syringe
it directly into her throat
    she sighs   falls back   the rickety bier is borne away to
                    the Alexanderplatz but not before
                            she calls '*Mein Herr*

    that insistent cough is due to you wearing my shift
in this coolest of antechambers   it leaves nothing to the imagination
    so the poem ends here'

The Spill

time slows then   accelerates   then again slows
either side of your coffee
its centrifugal milk-swirl
centred on a white table   everything else a peripheral blur
including Shadwell
it might look like Robert Smithson's *Spiral Jetty*
as seen from a high glider
if someone is up there
    having shinned a filter-elm

    to gain this aerial view
through a slit in the bowed striped awning
    and is noting the pool of sugar in your palm
        early morning mist as the smoke that comes off
of poured sugar
        you both awake and yawning

    the table so rickety   you rickety also
        just a microsecond before you propped one leg with
            a novella or this half-written poem on folded A4
you spilt the coffee
    the stain looking 'somewhat like a salt lake in Utah'
or so says a passing stranger
        apropos of nothing

Wispy Streamers

    supposedly Willem de Kooning
steps through   then beyond himself
through strip-door tassels
into an interior
of glare   murk and   yes   more variegated strip-door tassels
or ticker tape shredding from a steamer
as it departs New York   he's engulfed
    by cantankerous crowds on the quay
            'Goodbye! Goodbye!'   they say

    waving him away   [the reverse of how he arrived]
themselves lost in thought
and mostly on mute   popping
            the odd champagne cork   too aware
    to lose it even after

    he loses it   mind blank but hand full of cunning
blood pumping through clueless vessels but
    he never thinks
      of stopping

Pabl Picass

(after Paul Éluard)

    fourthly   it is the kind of a day that begins
with filter-elms crowding together
under heavy rain
the kind of day on which you had planned to be sad
then pretend that it's a surprise
when you are   a day when
someone just has to say 'arsehole!'
at the inappropriate funeral
heavy on the *langue* and *parole*
of it all
on that kind of day   you go in search of someone
whose fingers have scrabbled in raw earth
to pull lilacs out of graves
who sees a child as it is born and
        at the mirror stage simultaneously
in the same smear   the kind of day
which confuses the eye with the ear
as these wild young girls
with their bi-identifying *Converse* trainers
and pierced navels
shown off to each other behind the Unity Chapel
    that kind of 'kind of' day
in which   you see their eyes in some dubious future
or dubious past as   as the eyes
of battered courtesans   in soil-dark corsets
    with malingering hair who cry
down the wrong side of their faces
a step beyond human limits
and as if that wasn't enough
this keyboard with its faulty keypad on 'o'
    types out nothing   maybe *pabl picass*
the kind of day for avoiding primates
swinging up high in the filter-elms
let's call them arseholes   *arseholes*
    but quietly   that kind of day

Aphid Says

I

say what you want but
it seems I have disappeared...
or maybe landed
on the Shard   sky my skin is
say anything untoward
as this sky flinches   below:
traffic lights   sucked lozenges   green
    a three-legged dog

    crosses the zebra
tick tick tick   we are mobiles
    made of minuscule frenzy

    specks outside closed laundrettes
circuits whirring   we
    are invisible   but hard

II

say what you want but
I might grow a beard
tickle your hand with its feelers
the traffic a herd
of unnameable colours
like tainted blood cells
on Unicorn Street
    where we are specks on your lung

    Pre-Cogs of your cough
we aphids must unite
    to hail the indivisible

    unit!   smaller than the small
say these CisHet males
    by the Retail Cash Outlet

III

say what you want but
we are sick of Spring
endless regeneration
as Interactive Option Systems
play 'a little Vivaldi'
cheaply as we wait for 'no'
under high-build   buff cloud shelves
    that unicorn seen

on Unicorn St   is shot [just outside *Aldi*]
we cause loss of plant vigour
    you know our cornicles grow

exponentially
we'd be less than a pin head
    if we knew what pinheads were

IV

say what you want but
you slather for aphid butt
tut tut   secretly
train your tongue buds to stipple
deposits of honeydew
either say 'cool' or 'awesome'
nearly all the time
    as our monuments topple

brush us tenderly
yet know we are asexual
    aphid titbits   so

our vulnerability
is merely metatextual
    too small to know we are dead

Canton for the Stranded

    be even-handed
with yourself   and your shadow self
the vows rescinded
    the word 'gap' and the word 'gulf'

    note the filter-elms
hung with aphid mobiles
up-lit by ATMs
    at night   that stretch limousine   toe to tail

    passing through lush rain
to wave it on by
with nothing to gain
    is its own soliloquy

    we all qualify
so share that solipsism
when you can   sunlight
    refracted through a prism

    I think J.G. Ballard
wrote a novel in which
someone lived entirely on a traffic bollard
    in conurbation east of Ipswich

    or at least he should have done
you stand at a still centre
where one searchlight of neon
    makes four pistils   spore from there

The Tickle

    supposedly   to bring two turtles
– two small lozenge-green turtles –
to the single mum
and her overawed daughter
carried in frock coat pockets under linden trees   through the streets
                of Le Marais and the Latin Quarter
    then across the Seine
shows more than a modicum
                of pluck and empathy
    but   beyond that   to also provide toothpicks

    so the little one can tickle
them under the carapace
    is the beautiful detail

    your reputation belies
volcanic eruption   followed by retreat
            from
    diurnal to crepuscular tendencies

I Conjured up a Horse

(after Jules Supervielle)

    by the drawing of a breath
or the exhaling of one   I have a curious condition
yet whatever   I conjured a horse
on a day when the wild gorse
went yellow at the tips   and the moon
was a hangover from last evening   if
there are those who possess no belief
I have no time to condone
we deal with much worse
those of us who are 'blessed'
to occasionally call forth a quadruped
out of ether   especially on Sundays
when the sycamores
let loose flotillas of sycamore spores
whirl and let fly
go acquainting themselves again
    with the earth's surface…

    if not a horse
then a boat   if not a boat
then maybe a horse
    it all must be kept…

    discrepancies must be addressed
I say: *a brazier is defined*
by its holes   without them
it would be but a barrel
but none take this quarrel
    seriously

    if they had my condition
they could warm themselves on
the very word 'brazier'
without any need of a fire
but the hangover

of the yellow-tipped gorse
the aforementioned moon
cannot draw their attention
    they have no curious condition

    of course   I will cheerfully admit
my horse could equally be
seen as a breath-cloud
prone to galloping doubt
and a breath-cloud at night   at that
quiet   quite literally breathing me out
be that as it may
I will ride mine over
    the sky

Lamantia Street

I

you have been pondering
your first failure at this height –
not looking back in wonder
blaming the run-up   not the flight
to not go blundering in
as a green initiate
saying 'cool' or 'do your thing'
oblivious to fate
and its machinations   being wrong
about most things   here is the start:
through chill rain one humid Spring
Vaporfly soles on the dirt
rainwater in the awnings
by Lamantia Street
fire hydrants and horse dung
fish smells from the market
the market sellers singing
'Come on ladies   c'mon ladies   one pound fish' [singing? –
more of a shout] which makes you check the sky out
one cloud in the shape of a lung
– pareidolia or what? –
[where a Roadman calls you 'peng'
and you see it as insulting]
with a type of lightning
always on alert
not your standard *Sturm und Drang*
only serving half the night but
– networked, multi-branched, forking –
as if the districts were split
and sorted randomly by its conniving
fingers   you had fought
your way   carefully dodging
these   so as not to be lit
up or recognised   hoping
for a circular route
past the ATMs

upskirting the filter-elms
to lead back to your lodgings
unobserved   there   nine neon-green parakeets
will take off from your window ledge   wings
as a book being rifled   shaken out
to find a hidden note   wrung
out of every last word   or so you thought
    as you flop on your cot   blinking

II

    you pick up the book   start-
led to find an actual note   start reading:
hey, green initiate
it says   *your one ambition on show –*
as this beetle crawls
inchingly on the blade side
of a marram grass
the two of us too
tensed for the monumental
noise of all we have shed is
to let the mind atrophy
    in a lush meadow

III

    later   you will be wondering
about the onset of night
[when a Roadman calls you 'leng'
you *still* see it as insulting]
why each parakeet is a blur
why everything ploughs under
and the scribbled neon says:
you will be the green initiate
again   on the fly   be pondering
your first failure
    at this height

The Scarf

supposedly   if I find you   I find you disappointing but
only in relation to my projected vision   if
you find me   you find me disappointing but
    only in relation to your projected vision

    these meet mid-air in collision
to form a screen you change behind

    to avoid this confusion
we should always assume
    a mild degree of evil in all people

    so   take your semi-translucent patterned scarf
some other detachable part of your apparel
    throw it over that bedside lamp shade

    see?   the lightbulb now is either a small owl
                    or a large owl-moth
fluttery imprisoned but   trying to be understood
    the whole scene degraded
                    but beautiful

from **Transmitter**

bay tree   your simple
difficult radiance
light dividing equally
down your slim length   sideways on
your feet   in this concrete plot
still   going nowhere
the HAND CAR WASH sign points out
your deranged domed head
as if we must plunge in hands
    to give a head massage   as

    Rimbaud and the sisters
not lice but itchy aphids
    made mad by kneading

    jittery mobile
of aphids by Nelson Street
    musical barbed wire   leaf and air

                        * * * *

    all set: hot coffee
avocado and bacon
baguette   and still you will note:
to avoid envy   easy
make all your friends exactly
the same as you   steal
God's breath   see back beyond him
the clearing   beget
yourself   avocado and
    bacon   hot coffee

    the tree opposite
who says   *has it come to this*
    discourse with a talking tree?

    deflects enmity
yet   shimmy your top leaf and
    all these powers charge   solar

                        * * * *

sap accruing weight
in your omni-foiled head
Green Afro   the sap
in each leaf   repression
coursing   as worn as   Jason Bourne
on the 115 bus   thus
the trope of the outsider
alive   believed dead
outgrown   who will parkour up
    the Shard   leap through it sideways

    but never emote   just nod
shards   [never say *shards*]
    of glass everywhere   sharp as

    your leaves but blunt
-er   as hatchback windows up-
    load cloud files   say   *you've gone*

                              * * * *

    to avoid envy
says the bay tree   *we bay trees*
are all the same size
aphids assigned equally
we accept and repel light
in equal measure
thus bay trees and paving stones
all in accordance
and give   mutual back rubs
    or at least on the surface

    take priority
in the prequel   before God
    made the mistake of this world

    then went into rehab
avoid envy   treat sun and
    rain as the same   run

                              * * * *

bay tree   bay laurel
laurus nobilis   sweet bay
group evergreen shrub
flowering time spring   for crowns
though this might not be a bay
it's just that I say
it is therefore   *it is*
a bay   my own sweet species
I named in the first garden
    for you – your navel undefiled

    by me   or anyone
innocence was original
    then   disporting a snakeskin belt

    and not much else   night
something slippery is   riled
    sky I go down on

                    * * * *

    to call your bole 'bole'
is overestimation
the eye following up beyond
your 'bole' and crown to
cerulean pollution
crisscrossed by plane trails
doubled with this smoking butt
there   by the grating
thrown out   not down   and missing
    as sparks fire cities   but yet

    into your taut leaves
something silvery arrives
    as fine-point drizzle

    fibre optic sleet
'bole'   the word's circumference
    is vast   not so your slim waist

                    * * * *

today Green Afro
you look forlorn   yet your twin
seems spry   water or
lack of it   parking meter
municipal bin   rubbish
bags   small chair with its
Styrofoam scar   which never
will note in whisper
the heights you essay:
     finding God is easy   try

     finding the still space before
God existed   sweet clearing
     where you might be enlisted

     God being this thought
three magpies peck the dirt   flirt
     then flutter   start for the sky

* * * *

     where we go from here:
the clearing   rarefied air
where Spring gives way to
snow line   beyond there   exhale
breath   to know you are still there
eyes?   somewhere between
here and heaven   height?   likewise
eyes [wood knots] sometimes
double as nipples   as when
     tree surgeons sex trees in spring

     we are all saplings
reliant on mesh support
     then   an upright prop

     this misprision
where we grow   are restrained
     equally   to gain this height

* * * *

I made a sundial
a sundial in Shadwell
– it seemed to lack one –
out of a bollard   and light
from the late-service laundrette
where I sat for hours
time a maximum load   *tick*
the smell of *Surf* on
the paving stones   counting cracks
    the sun   seething at ease

    its spin circle as
the turn of the universe
    as laundrettes are clocks

    a monument   self-made of
washing grains and will   please   please
    don't bump into my sundial

                              *   *   *   *

    first: go meet with God
second: see through him   if a
him   to this clearing
some small space off Turner Street
replete   with laurel   dustbin
bags   parking meter
street cleaners in livery
yellow flak jackets
mostly   then   small luxury
    bacon and avocado

    baguette   Americano
with milk   hot   rickety table
    two sugars   the devil's work

    start to think of
falling   falling   and swerving
    third: at the last minute   brake

                              *   *   *   *

the day is taking
its time   to shrew-grey from lime-
yellow   lost freeze frame
of a furred-over city
frayed   the bay tree seems steel
whereas the night is a pelt
of fur light and manhole steam
rising willow-tobacco
extra mellow? slow
    ingraining the kerbstones   so

    the night comes down
as a see-through condom slid
    on in some *Novotel*

    naiad or dryad?
this being the first rumour
    someone tomorrow will tell

* * * *

    of this small snail and
its glutinous   brown-veined haul
we must make mention
its attempt up your left side
careful   luminous antlers
give nothing away
of the will   low-wattage will
whist you   preening   oblivious
feel another wood knot   moving
    carry on as normal   though

    the land is moving
break   break   breaking up
    Mitteleuropa   luminous antlers

    which crawl towards your crown
who will give vent?
    who grants this slowness sanction?

* * * *

'semi-conductor'
they say   'omni-conductor'
I say   quite briskly
'sepal oscillator'
today   all leaf edge   and byte
Intel incoming
wind direction   light
demagogue's conference speech
from The Capital   *Lidl-*
    bag   megahertz   trip-hop

    you humming somewhere
in a bathroom   curtain-blurred
    tune unmistakeable

    I will tune this dial
of light-struck leaf   reach *white noise*
    anything but you   happy

                                    * * * *

    the most reluctant
will occasionally consent
through boredom   not want
to be slightly caressed in
a partially clad fashion
as if on a divan
though there is   in fact   no divan
then   having come   will busy
themselves in some
    cause   some cause or other but

    never mine though   never mine
today   our bay tree is nervous
    bright   shivery as

    if witness to thwarted love
as one asked in as alibi
    who cannot find the right lie

                                    * * * *

you're a study for
Nude with Green Bath Towel on Head
Giacometti's
quick preliminary sketch
your body is this one line
a lost *meisterwerk*
you got shampoo in your eyes
wood knots?   remember?
see your terrible shyness
   as you step from the shower

   into Turner Street
the passing dustbin men shocked
   at dank pubic hair

   slunk into gutters
one bay leaf   body gel bubbles
   gone   spilt into Bollo's Brook

                  * * * *

   laurel   circular
wreath made of interlocking
branches   leaves of the
bay laurel   aromatic
broad leaf evergreen   later
from spineless butcher's broom or
Ruscus Hypoglossum   i.e.
[*Caesar's crown*]   not here
ragged sapling   seeming street corner
   fly-girl-boy   a   ne'er-do-well

   impenetrable
defences   and mostly gone
   head a horseshoe

   of pungent sensi
who lies   'I am Petrus Borel or Jeanne Duval
   got the gear?   show us, son'

                  * * * *

    bay tree   bosom friend
you are my reliable
unstable yourself
though you be   *anything penned*
is only the end result
of the force behind
it   remember that?
your heavy top leaf
under this fair-weather sun
    is brilliant   bastion

    even in stiff wind
unlike certain some   who fray
    pliant   don't face the question

    but let it rankle
before resurfacing   my
    Achilles heel   your –

                    *   *   *   *

    Pataphysicians
working through the night know that
revision is right
six revisionary
ratios – for example –
are ample   the least employed
any working day   my café
stealthily reducing my-
self until nothing is spared
    hard   fifty-seven years   hard

    a bay could shed sepals
enough to litter this road
    with a mother lode   yet

    to afford one oval
of shade for a lone aphid
    is enough reward

                    *   *   *   *

take this paving stone
unseen   make it go airborne
for revolution
then the next one   the next one
followed by a thick kerbstone
says this slim bay tree
not usually given
to fronting a megaphone
take down the towers of stone
with stone from their foundations

as ants in the join
of the paving stones under–
mine its grouting   go outing

the unsure   only pedants
abstain   take down the moated
astrodomes   we are the ants

* * * *

so: these two bay trees
this many metres apart
on the pavement   will soon sway
their top levels brighten   shown in
the sun   their darker lightens
somehow in vision
though vision is just not done
I will see them at the end
walking arm in arm
across this pavement   *stay calm*

I am over them
the sky is not separate
nor day yet from night

– the details here not quite clear –
yet they keep each other from
harm   and I am over them

* * * *

what is the use of
yielding to the numinous
if the numinous
keeps all the light? says
the bay   quite offhandedly
stars so hard they burn   apart
distant and magnificent
yet give light   gratuitously
and always too late
    for the receivers

    then it hits this spoon
with no little ignition
    and it stirs   milk swirls

    silver tables   milk-
whorls   circle within circle
    a plate seen from satellite

                              * * * *

    someone broke the world
Schopenhauer would say it
was God   who else?   but
others lay claim and haggle
for the prize   overtly bent
amongst the rubble
this bay tree in anxious flail
shivering inside   bathed in
translucent octagons of
    blue light   passing police vans

    down Commercial Road
some crazy in *McDonald's*
    giving utter vent

    waving a fake sword
wild   invoking God   any God
    and the coffee not yet cold

                              * * * *

being a bay tree
meshed/clamped   pole-pinioned out
by pavement and sky
the world won't level with me
this   this rectangle of light
blinks and delimits
if you see a lone magpie
twice   it is sorrow seen twice
if I see a lone magpie
    twice   it is joy   once

    and longing   for three
but friends   when I straighten out
    determine this height   survey

    wimps and minions!
one metre ninety   only
    great champions can clear me

                         * * * *

    bay tree   you slight tease
out in inclement weather
slighting me always
anyone can stand outside
as though preternaturally
calm   sometimes we must
put forth   your body slim
as avoidance   your head full
of seething   with all you cannot
    say   I could grant you some lines

    but they would not translate
unless in strophes of green light
    turning grey on slate

    like rain does   endless
sublimation can only
    give birth to [too] late   to night

                         * * * *

   to submit to rage
now   would hurt at least seven
other people   so all to
play for   Green Afro   warn me
off   douse me in your green calm
I would touch you in
at least nine different places
Rimajov for one   Streatham
mist lower than the mountain
   a nightshirt struggled out of

mother in heaven
blue bolt of time   of satin
   neither spur   nor balm

   every day the litany – *one aspirin and one statin* –
O my dear sweet bay   even our memory foam
   mattress has forgotten us

          * * * *

   and you say such things:
when a snail eats another
snail it inherits
its memory   when a wasp
eats another wasp it gains
ESP   that I
ate one bay leaf and turned in-
to a young bay tree
forgetting everything
   bitter edge   raw   drying sedge

   yet the bay is so
big-headed   it believes it
   ought to stop a drought

   one leaf   lying there
comfortable   outmoded
   in the propped maw of a trout

          * * * *

the young!   so assured
so expensive   so shallow
so clipped   copper-plated
that they do not know   beauty
their own   unknowing also
super-alluring
to essay innocence [and plagiarised often the essay]
so sullen they do
not even see   this bay tree
    it too being prinked   partitioned

    semi-cold   corralled
in mesh   so networked
    behind   so multi-channelled

    so wired-up   so stalled
so aglow with semi-love
    delimited   still   they grow

                    *   *   *   *

    see: this well of shade
out of which grows a sapling
shade intravenously
taken in   by osmosis
making its sepal-tips dark
or darker   or that's just evening
coming on   only the froth-glow
off your Americano
to illuminate nearby
    as a brief acetylene spark

    its ellipse   its moon
in part-eclipse   if we right   [or wrong]
    the picture plane   to see by

    to find an oasis inside a desert   turn
left [or right]   go past Spring   by
    Turner Street   into Shadwell

                    *   *   *   *

O heart   over-used
beating for a bay tree's bole
too tough   pumped wood knot
this heart is convoluted as
a curtal sonnet   writ
in the ink of an aphid's
subliminal noise
full   reaching the ears
coffee defibrillators
    tick in trochaic metre

    under my left nipple   still
try listening to it
    how it pines when satisfied

for less than   for more than
how satisfied with pining
    without which   it would not [wood knot] beat

* * * *

    if the bonds of friendship hold
which they rarely do
their value decreasing [as] our
futures enlarge   surge
as the massed banks of cloud
the edge of which are   grey-gold?
mostly   a rare sight
if the bonds of friendship hold
separation   does not dim
    influence   flooding back   in

    yet if one half is withheld
then the breast goes numb
    touch   once warm   will scald

    O my bosom friend   the friendless are a
sickly guild   we draw on blood
    if the bonds of friendship hold

* * * *

    argue hot evening
overhead   pressure mounting
foliage frothy-thick
tower blocks   these light-layers of
arguing couples
in kitchens   bedrooms   *go fuck your lip salve from Holly's*
but   my argument is with
everyone   with God if
there was one   with foliage
     aphids   tower blocks   bricks   Spring

     especially
those who come   placatory
     with tissues   lectures

     lies   conjecture   night
refusing to take sides with day
     argue on   hot evening

                              * * * *

     sensing trees at night
weight of frothy overhang
pressuring the mind
no boles   no branch   no exit
invisibility's weight
– the strain put on art to solve inequality
or signify solving it   alibi for inaction
as the state withdraws –
leaving a city of silt
     [this park a dropped scarf]

     but try not to dwell on it
you can't name trees in the dark
     splints   genus   species

     nor can you sex them
accurately   this bay tree
     by the low-lit park   this breeze

                              * * * *

    see this: from inside your mouth
issues a thin green sapling
pinioned   bound in mesh
you can taste its scale of shade
fading at the edge   of circumference
– where Shadwell might start –
centrifugally ripple outwards
almost beyond sense
the city radiating
    out   beyond even itself

    as from The East to The South
as if trees could walk
    never mind talk   your mouth

    holds a sour bay tree pip
that bursts through your palette   up
    up into your head   then out

                                        * * * *

    so call this a *pause*
replenishment   exhaustion
not *your* exhaustion
the years before   quester's fire
and it's not yet 7.00 a.m.
under an awning
yawning   call me the Prince of
Tyre or   maybe don't
born of a Shadwell bus ride
    to this roughshod thoroughfare

    the masses opine
a lover pulls out mid-fuck
    steam escapes an *Xpelair*

    fondles this kerb and
I try prising gifts [back]   from lack
    praying to be unaware

                                        * * * *

neither of us smokes
unless we smoke this afterglow   to properly rest
in a true *post-coital tristesse*
– stucco as the inner-city's blossom –
and slowing breath   the
filaments of all four lungs
as trees   opening   closing their buds
exhaling smoke rings   as if
we told the time
   by inhaling exhaust fumes

   both of us are dead
laid out next to each other
   one hand   bent over backwards   barely touching one hand

   and yes   I know you're a wraith
a bay tree   a wreath
   discordant   perfect   always the best wake

* * * *

   chagrin   *Squibs/ Rockets*
nothing but the night's dank lung
table-candle guttering
these square-lit top deck faces
pass   think they own the night   right?
forgetting that we own *them*
sat by borrowed beer bottles
our glaze   our sprockets
of 16mm film   bus-brushed filter-elm
   [so slim they called you *nothing-butt*]

   us who duck under
the arc of sensor-arches
   rather than vine trellises

   we who walk through screens
hooded by white noise   *search us*
   our bay tree blurs its own face

* * * *

if you shoot   shoot straight
talk is   monosyllables
full frame this bay tree
close on rain-stippled sepals
hold for a while   then edit
Cassavetes says
character is time   and time
properly handled   is film
the bay not the elm
    get the right fucking species!

Cassavetes cries
dialogue is   monologue
    colour is a lie

    see in black and white
lack is right   parking meters
    tick   says Cassavetes   *cut*

* * * *

I will put you on
feel the weight distribution
gone awry   my arms in your sleeves
sleeves of sinuous tissue   [one spare rib for the Maker]
their colours strange   as
the colour-blind see   colour
O roundness where hardness
was   and my cock gone
my voice up an octave   gives
    some fluent honey-release

[as does elsewhere]   as
does Chet Baker when
    he summons that swoon   to sing

    as my mind turning
to men   a numb conundrum   [Chet – the little shit]
    I am the green bay   I am a woman

* * * *

61

they are laying the bay tree
the length of three paving stones
the great Green Afro
flattened at the back
lain straight
somewhere just off Turner Street
three council workmen
are they re-potting?   see their
backs strain   green drumlins   Spring rain
  so fine it's invisible

  as you tend to be
our shy figure for a tree
    seeing these tired lovers   heavy petting

  who put one wet finger
against the centre
    as eyelids   bay leaves   simmer

* * * *

Undescended Testicles

decide to stay put
avoid The Hanging Gardens
the wind chimes tilting
in the blue fir   the women
    wielding their fans   silk rustling

utterly content
a pine cone's complications
    are enough   it's rough out there

The Obligations

though I have never met you
but sense you out there
   on open ground
   waving slightly   stretching against a tree
      I might draw you in
         through telepathy

   to proffer both my hands
in greeting
   though you are merely
   a fleeting   a sprite   yet
      despite these ethers these   zinc buffers
         this offer to you still stands

   if late at night   the filter-elms are green
and staining the ATMs
   with their grey-green filigree
   so you cannot read
      the numbers
         that demand

   the entirety of the funds
you do not have
   [for a small handling fee]
   as the city sinks to silt
      despite all such clearances
         or not   my offer to you still stands

   I know nothing about you
palpably less   maybe
   so if   in public gardens
   park keepers resign
      then flee
         leaving slashed growbags   cans

of paraquat and hooch
some glimpsing trellises   some
   see-through diamonds
   of air   as if for free
      despite this choice between apparitions
         my offer to you still stands

   if your neighbour toils
diligently
   to undermine you
   soiling the wavebands
      with calumny and spite
         though you showed him your open hand

   you might yet rely on me
– slowly learning to live without ulterior motive –
   to rescue your soul
   [I do not lack ambition]   proffer a hand
      the gargantuan reach or the tiny
         despite the toil   the times

   my offer to you still stands

Double-hooped Earrings

O help me to find my bearings
in the unstable dialectic between 'presence' and 'absence'
　　[hereafter represented by my double-hooped earrings]
　　'so piratical!' they aver　　'such decadence!'
　　　as if my double-hooped earrings
　　　were the two 'o's in 'oomph'
　　that level of erudite reference
　　but　　of course　　the holes have opened up after multiple wearings
opened up the dialectic between 'presence' and 'absence'
　　so I see only after-trace　　the corona of two ball bearings
　　in eclipse　　a glint　　an ice cube　　my whole being tensed
between skewer and pulpy lobe　　I guess I am frightened　　I guess
　　we bear such things
　　for vanity　　vanity and the biting wince
of pain　　pain precedes my double-hooped earrings
　　　then follows up as the butterfly is tightened around the dialectic
　　　　between 'presence' and 'absence'

　　yet after　　I wince down a flight of ringed stairs
out into light and suddenly sense
　　that as mere things precede us in time　　outlive us　　our fate is
　　　　　　　　　　　　　　　　　　　putrescence
　　　　to exist between 'presence' and 'absence'

　　　wherein we find our bearings　　if sincerity undermines this poem
is one of its many failings
　　so too　　I guess　　does the decadent glint
　　　of my double-hooped earrings

The Unbalanced

I
recently   in hospital
coming off some pill
I misplaced an earring and
being thin   felt unbalanced
    leaning more to the left side

each weight needs a counterweight

II
in bed   you lie to my right
a tangle of sheet   a hand
out of which I extrapolate
the whole   restored later   by light
    and gravity's pull

[ellipse of glass on nightstand]

III
I will tell you one thing
this lack is like
the sound of the wind whistling
through an earring   or worse
    through the hole where the earring was

I have been shaved and slit

    still   we proceed by erring

Unicorn Street

I

    to abandon wizardry
is to instigate   a sick fern season so dry
any fen goes slate
under the slate canopy
abandon the star-pilot
and his mazy itinerary
see existence without plot
    or existence as hearsay

    until clarity
wells up like light   wizardry's
    after-trace can then multiply

    to initiate thought
in the thoughtless initiate
    it starts with a cut

II

    it starts with a cut
right across that wizard's wrist
– line of livid white –
to cut that wizard open
to see his entrails ripen
to see what spills out
eviscerated heart
    like a bunched and opening fist

    toxic sky-dust   guts
presumably we
    think all wizards' last

    but they all go out
into that pre-planned   nail-filled blast
    abandoning pointy hats

III

    all those pointy hats
with pointy heads inside them
            full up from the brim
make for blunt thoughts   thoughts
of abandoning the realm
– retail cash outlets
dappled by the filter–elms
on Unicorn Street
    fake frontage for a film

    that will never make the cut
wobbling   fazed   flimsy –
    the thoughtless initiate will first disembowel
             the wizard   then cut the wizard's throat

    hold the voice box tight
in their lacerated palm   then
    kick off down Unicorn Street

The Confessional

supposedly   whilst shaving my left nipple
well   around my left nipple   – we all have our vanity –
I slipped   nicked myself
to make a pert blood-bubble
semi-translucent
with bathroom windows in it
curved sheen 'C's of mercury
    how I wish you would sense it

    approach in silence
            and suckle
with your cool mix of spite and solemnity
            to get your very first fix

    to draw forth my soul
        with your blowsy mouth
lick the trickle down my chest
    that will soon rust my belt buckle

    take down whole districts
                like any variant
blights an entire continent
    with drought and pestilence until
            somehow we ride this one out

from The Drifting Recidivist Says

I

as   of course   the urge
to shock is an invalid start
to any work of art
– though passable as by-product –
so is to tickle the tear duct
or hide in the abstract
nothing will supplant the fact
    that the sea is topaz   especially saying it is

    it's a spectrum in phase
the mimetic merely dilutes the surge
    of it   gun-grey to chrysoprase

    thence to the leaden   so   finally   lies are forged
Laforgue it was who first used the word 'clitoris'
    in a line of verse

II

Charlie B: as we assimilate
everything love has taught us
– uplifting this, repressing that –
but assimilating none the less
you might presume
my gift – a gemstone on a slivery chain
to hang around your neck –
    would uplift your fear   repress your pain

    or be a charm for luck
as if the sultry essence of your scent
    could be distilled within it

whilst I would not have the heart
to tell you   'this is the last of the original stones
                    des Esseintes used
    to suffocate his tortoise'

71

III

clairaudience: I still hear you speaking
the illusion solid
as a flash of lightning
because to eavesdrop the dead
is simply a commonplace
the acoustics of your pad   suggest a baroque fireplace
a full set of tungsten tongs
   – *multi-channel   omni-channel* – but

   I see a herd of reindeer
bend to nuzzle reindeer moss
   their antlers crackling

   with radioactivity
in a lichen-filled crevasse –
   they have nothing to tell me

IV

   supposedly   you catch me urinating
into a space helmet on
the crust of the planet Charon
– a yellow curvature of piss
an orange curvature of horizon –
as our flag ripples
with the backdraft of an auroral storm
   that looks at us merely in passing

   then sweeps on   ripe apples hang
from an invisible tree
   as stars swerve and hover

   then blink out   a.m. one little pill
followed by another little pill p.m.
   my suit a dinted blister pack
               left on a breakfast table

V

    dear   get over it
the impasse   or the unsaid
will accrue as moss
on manholes your damaged world
tap tap   the lines you skip
the lure of the white rectangle's
interminable intel
    smothering the bluff   scree freed

    as asterisks in email   finger in crevice
Facebook   pack ice   *Skype*
    the baffle of the crevasse

    hang because of cowardice
stay because of cowardice
    please   but hang or stay

VI

    deliquescence: as spring
in blossom   either I am a changeling
or my mother has taken many lovers
in place of my father
pulling them to her bosom
along with the odd maidservant   in a lather
of dopamine   gel and eucalyptus
    thus

    is the sky-dome over
my life   the elongated shade that strikes out from the colosseum
    way past the clover

    leaf interchange down to the sea's hem
to you fuckbuddy   up to your calves in the boiling surf
    one cinder of which is enough

Plume Travelling

(after Henri Michaux)

   so Plume cannot say
he has been treated right when travelling
some pass right through him without a word of warning
They wipe their hands on his coat   it is but a thing
They serve him a root   un-courteously   he will say
   'what a very big root!
a very big root
on my plate!'   but eat
and eat in all modesty   as if not at all in a sty
and if
at night They refuse him a room   refuse Plume!
saying   you have come so far for a bed?
take your knapsack and   stick your crust of stale bread   and head
for the roads
sleepwalkers like you can have no need of a bed
and Plume will say   politely   'OK!
it was just my little joke
this need for a permanent bivouac'
and be on his way
at last light into   the dead of night
and similarly if
They throw him out of a boxcar
saying   again you have come too far
to sleep on a cargo of coal is too much luxury   They say
   this train ushers a spume
of choking smoke all night   burning bright   it plots its course but not
for the likes of Plume
then he will say   'Ahem, OK'
and jump out into the night
and if at the Colosseum
in Rome
where the lions are keeping *stumm*
The Cloakroom Attendants will say   to Plume
be on your way!   this place is crumbling

already   it's flaking away   if you stay
it might collapse completely
for who is in need of History?   it makes us numb
Plume be gone!
and Plume will say
    'Yes Sir I do concur!
who needs a postcard when I can see this far!'
and go   the invisible traveller
and likewise when
on a riverboat The Purser will point at Plume and say
– as they pass those unsettled banks of nettle and sallow –
he might inflame the crew
and impute a mutiny!   take him down below
the second watch has rung!
before he blinks   have him walk the plank
Plume has   already by then   jumped overboard   whistling
to swim   as the current allows
the moon like the capital 'O'
on a faulty keyboard
later drying
he will say nothing
will Plume
being
utterly aware
by the night docks   the boon docks
and the low lights of the river
of what all his fellow travellers have to bear
    no   Plume will do nothing   but sing

The Bungalow

I

   will think about stairs
very little else but stairs
even occasionally
a spiral staircase
vast   lit up like a modernist corkscrew
– but not though the waterfall –
mostly it's horizontal here
   or more than horizontal

II

   'did you bring your furbelow?'
you usher from a side room
– voice so full-frontal –
draped   a red feather boa
winding about you like a spiral staircase
   very little else   out there

III

   six or maybe seven wind-slanted trees rise
         from a lush meadow
of vetiver   vetiver   lemongrass and citronella
half the moon on fire
far off a twister   something like a spiral staircase
preparing for a sweep-through
here   *Night Wings*   *Always* propped
on the piping in the rudimentary loo
the white sound of the
moon above resinous firs
bleaching the sheets of
the other house guests
on heavy air   a feather   very little else
   I trip on a stage prop

'Baby   let's go upstairs'

'But we live in a bungalow'

'I meant it as a metaphor'

   'Oh.'

Horse in the Sea Mist

I

   bumping into you
was very much like   bumping into a
horse in the sea mist
[or a security door at night]
a grey-maned   grey-forelocked horse
looming out of foehn
out of grey-forelocked   grey-maned micro-mist
suddenly so solid-bodied
that you shudder at size and scale
[and no this is not an advert]
the great battering ram of
the brow   star-burned   the colossal hind parts
soon your own brow is star-burned
the nostrils twin road tunnels
the scent preceding
yet with those   yearning chrome-brown eyes
as if turning up at a tryst
the jawbone scribbled with kelp
sargassum and fauve-brown bladderwrack
an enemy of mistrust
in all its snuffling quiddity
the swiftest of shocks   as it farts and says:
   '*my sweetness   be calm*
I will always reserve the right
to emerge from dullness in–
to light   at a time you least expect
even though my scent precedes me   usually
this shock is always renewable
now halter me to that length
of fraying cable...give me those meds
plus stroke my mane
   to untie all the knots...'

you peek and see that
the cable you halter your horse to
   is green-speckled with rust

II

'all of this eavesdropped –
the 'eavesdrop' is patently
bust as an art   done
due to a decline in eaves
   and the rise of personal headphones'

'that is, Matthew'   the horse said
'apart from prolix quadrupeds
   no one is listening'

III

I came around the corner
of Beverstone and Leander Roads
at a rate of knots
[where a drain above the Effra
linked us to the sea
tangentially]   around that corner
so fast the decade changed
to bump   smack-bang right into you –
I had been   so   smack-bang   into you
though you smoked then only a bong –
yet here you were wreathed   again   in sea mist
your forehead scorch-burned
grey-forelocked   grey-maned micro-mist
with yearning chrome-brown eyes
as if in a tryst
we nearly collided
yet narrowly missed each other
   on that hairpin curve   yes   narrowly missed

IV

    somewhere   in all of this
– the chronology went astray –
in a slanted shack
near a pine-scented sea coast
an overloaded mare
pained and seemingly indifferent
to the miracle
drops two foals in their glycerine bags
onto a sump of warming straw
the afterbirth like micro-mist
like twin roads glistening
as time extends and lags
you peek to see they both have
star-burnt brows as they
totter up on collapsing
tripod legs   then   start zero
    -ing in on her scent

This Pure Child

(after Jules Supervielle)

then this innocent child
pops out   product of a wild and filthy fuck
one night of sin distilled
to a sweet open rose
new as luck is new   can such disruption chill
chill us out?   no   it gives birth to our hearts
not previously involved   stowaway in the cradle
    we charge you with assault

    assault and battery by   such little fists
we are kneed in the groin   by your puckered knees
the mirage-like loom bands of
    your wrists   that centrifugal
            swirl about your fontanelle

    bulbous belly holding no malice as
we tightly guard this secret
    this secret   that everybody knows

The Height

here at the height of my powers
I feel so tired
as if beyond the snow line
and so give in   retreat   lie on the snow
under Alpine larch   hard-stemmed long Brac fir
                        or Pinyon pine
the pain in my shins
here at the height of my powers   noticing
    even in Spring   even in snow   you now
                            turn a naked back

bare as Tibetan cypress or Chinese juniper where
everything that isn't   happens in between solidities
            makes these trees shake

invisible snow showers   the inverse of blossom
        these flying houses of stucco –
in the rarefied air   my head becomes light   I feel so tired
            here at the height of my powers

Star-wheel

they are going well   your latest attempts to be shallow
to watch knowledge dilute   to a clear
fathomable goo
   on a need-to-know basis

or rather   a need-to-*not*-know   all surface   thin cover of snow
under which Spring is   maybe   here
they are going well
   your latest attempts to be shallow

there is nothing you need to know
no thought indeed   no thesis [thank God]   no fear
of impending anything
   just a fashionable need-to-know basis

of whatever this is   being all that there is
and to try to prove otherwise is   to become a mere
fool   though a knowledgeable fool   who is not doing well
   in their latest attempts to be shallow

a career?   a slalom-slippage   a career?
a crazy figure of eight on an ice-thin lake   whoa!
a slither   a fast furthering
   of crisis following crisis

so   wobble purposefully   never try to steer
whichever greatest star-wheel seems in reach   instead   try to know
less   shoo in the Spring   *find the desert inside the oasis*
                achieve the banal
   O they are going well   your latest attempts to be shallow

Fusillade

'the next fusillade
of catkins   buckshot or   slate
either windfall or
scattershot   is expected
at any particular
second   a wince of foresight
to pierce pin holes in the night
  make of it a colander'

I said   with all the
rigor of a QAnon influencer
on a blocked social media platform
'God grant me peace   or if not
  at least an unruly truce'

as my shoulder burst
with exit wounds of blossom
  as the sky bared its stars and said

'waiting is tiresome
not for nothing do I dread
  the next fusillade'

Canton for the Wastrel

so much is wasted
— I thought I was the wastrel —
time   wheat-stalks   crickets
crickets welded to wheat-stalks
near the birch thicket   remember that?   then
that horsetail waterfall
a nymph of the river's source
fresh but bitter when tasted
in brackish rivulets   gone way off course
as the faux-naive prove   actually naive
and freshets bring no
reprieve   even this full Spring
there's scattershot hail
at wincing windows though   my long face is only
my resting face thankfully

propped up on this sill
surveying the field below
with some considerable
skill   and not much grace
I stake out my position   too shallow to fail
so: easy to give advice
useless and exact   my sweet
harder to subtract —
at the very moment when
the angle of the peak sun
makes a deeper trough of each furrow
[ironically golden]
in their taut converging lines —
yes   harder to subtract   queasy blue sorrow
and disassociation from your heart and brow

worth trying though

Depot of the Aero-houses

I

  in spite of ourselves
we could always imagine
somehow ending up at the
depot of the Aero-houses
invisible though they were
behind a copse of filter-elms
linked fencing and foreground hedgerows
blinding us from the road
that full, curious droning
as if the first bees of spring
                 were massing
around the heads of the whisker-wheat
but much amplified
a drone that vibrated the mind
if not the foundations of the
the Aero-houses
where much was incoming   much outgoing
that we could only sense ourselves
as if under cloud cover
coming through at low levels
signed by spurious batmen
between the rows of lights
that ran parallel then fused
            into a mess of dropped jewellery
or taupe-fauve frogspawn
  as we stopped before the fencing

II

  if a house flies
it flies high and flies heavy
its jagged undercarriage of masonry
and trailing cable
vast and shading the ground beneath
shading then moving on

outing small startled voles
darting red-eyed as if beneath lightning
smell and sight become improvised guides
if a house flies
    it flies heavy and high

III

    waiting for the pass over
the fly-by   we counted six varieties of vine
we counted aphid mobiles
under the filter-elms
itchy with thorn and bite
a dock leaf as a gramophone horn
hedgerows staying resolute as
we strained up at moving cloud shelves
and undulant isobars
    as the patterns on a huge sole
'Jesus!' said Beatrice 'Fuck!' said Dan 'it's time!'
we looked at our shoes
at glutinous snail trails
of the route from whence we had come
glistening backwards
and knew we would never now approach the
depot of the Aero-houses
    in spite of ourselves

The Weathervane

(after the Czech of Karel Toman)

    a dilapidated squat   in the wall–
cracks creeping moss   dewlapped mushrooms   tick-infested lichen chill
out or doze   in the yard
nettles hustle bindweed
in a tangle   the ornamental fountain that Lee
and Vags once fell in is overrun   the slashed tree
full of apple blight and lightning
    that cannot remember when it was hung

    with blossom   though on clear days   to be fair   linnets
rustle and whistle and on sunny days
    the gable's weathervane

    begins to spin in
time   its creak singing to the heat haze
    somewhere between joy and pain   everything
                            is camouflage

Bollo's Brook

if you would follow
Bollo's Brook like a light blue
vein below the skin
of the city   say southwards
   its gurgle beneath your feet

   this hot Spring *Tarmac*
as a spasm up the spine
yet low on the mind
these will be your only guides:
   three tutelary swallows

   tracking it   wedged there
behind their satellite dish
nested temporarily
to mimic-sing its onrush
   song of forgotten rivers

   unheard through gutter-spars
circled by nitrous oxide
cylinders   induced
laughter from last night's youngsters
   who vanish at 5.00 a.m.

   – all this in its song –
then you have a new pathway:
from Ealing Common
hard along the District Line
   flowing south through Turnham Green

   to drain in the Thames
downstream of Barnes Bridge   the edge
where you now loiter
fingering a blister pack
   of Paracetamol   still

    still   you would follow
a windblown strip of tinfoil
negotiating
gutters in your current state
    the Parliament of Foil

    idly presiding
air ordnance   policy by wish
primped-up advisors
advising more advisors
    thus   the source of the headache:

    a drifting dead swan
royally protected   neck
in a taut reef knot
split gut full of millet   one
    webbed foot rotted in the reeds

    and a crown of flies
you lie downstream of the stink
cinquefoil   rushes
crushed on the bank   and wait
    for the government to fall

    to fall in step with
this too tangible dray horse
down a bridle path
as six psycho-geographers
swerve   satnavs on the blink by

    eel caravans as
Francesca da Rimini [in neon-green cargo pants]
                tugs hard at the rein
but still strokes the nose
soft nostrils   twin road tunnels
    fragrant with sorrel and tar

mul- or dewberry
frothing like an aria
by the link fencing
where this horse plaited with thyme
   trit-trots the South Circular

* and likewise you will follow*
Bollo's Brook like a light blue
vein below the skin
of the city   say southwards
   its feint   garbled song your fate

The Lynx

who feels a thought for
quite inexplicable reasons
– no FLOW-MATIC compiling   emoticon camouflage –
who lopes on this thin sand-spit
as ribbed ferns conduct   lint-snags of lightning
through six turbulent seasons
                            of dust and pack ice
who remains taut   taut in the nape-fur   for
    a mistral off Malabar

    or some freak incoming wind   who tends her litter
starts practising sortilege
    to tend them in their future

    yet retains such grace
                            as lightning retains its sting
with lynx cubs under a Nerium oleander   that
    I must step back to see her

accidentally   to tread a starfish
further down into hot sand
startle   pick it up
one of only two starfish
– the five tines of any wish –

on which all your hopes are pinned:
the one you have in your grip
*   the one left there in the ground*